JOURNEY
of a SOUL

JOURNEY
of *a* SOUL

JOHN-ROGER

MANDEVILLE PRESS
Los Angeles, California

Published by Mandeville Press
P.O. Box 513935
Los Angeles, California 90051-1935
323/737-4055

email: servicedesk@msia.org
Printed in the United States of America

ISBN: 978-1-893020-13-9

Visit us on the Web at www.mandevillepress.org

CONTENTS

1
The JOURNEY BEGINS

In the beginning of time, God was in all places in an absolutely pure state. And in this purity, It was a void—without specific consciousness. In essence, God did not know Itself, in awareness, in Its greater beingness. So God instituted patterns of creation. It created universes, within which was what appeared to be solid objects (which we call planets) and less solid material (which we call space). All of it is God in Its different manifestations. And God instituted the plan that every part would know every other part—through experience. Thus the Soul, which is more directly the spark of God, was evolved and was given the opportunity to experience all levels, layers, planes and realms of experience and being. A Soul can inhabit any form it wishes. Its job, its reason for being, is to experience all it can on every level it can—thereby growing in awareness of its own divine nature. The

Soul that has experienced all is God and is one with God. This experience of God is incomprehensibly large and complex, so the Soul spends tremendous time evolving through the realms of experience back into the awareness and knowledge of its divine nature.

Let me give you an idea of this by telling you a story about a Soul that decided it would leave heaven—the Soul realm. It got a little bored one day so it said to itself "Thou art a rock." And sure enough, it was a rock. It got in a little bit of trouble because it found itself isolated; there weren't any other rocks nearby, and it couldn't move around very much. But this Soul was pretty happy anyway because the nature of the Soul is joyful. The rock was heavier than anything else around it, so it kept sinking into denser areas until it came to the place called Earth. It settled down with a slight jolt and said, "Oh, wow, I really am this rock." It didn't know what to do next, so it said, "I think I'll learn patience." And it sat there for a long time.

Over the course of thousands of years, the rock slowly eroded and broke apart. Then the Soul said, "That's interesting. I'm freer now." But it wasn't too free because it found out that it had been absorbed into the land, and now it was being absorbed into a tree. That was a little better than being the rock. At least it could play in the sun and enjoy the breeze—and it really felt fantastic. It thought, "This is great; I'm really having a wonderful experience. I think I've learned patience being a rock. Now I think I'll learn gradualness." So it was part of the tree for a long time, until one day it decided to become the fruit on the tree.

The fruit became ripe in its time, and it fell down and decayed. Then there appeared a worm who lived off the fruit; and pretty soon the worm sprouted wings and discovered it could fly. And the Soul said, "Wow, that's pretty good. I've learned patience and gradualness, and now I just have to learn elevation." So it flew around, but as it flew, it found out that a bird came along and absorbed it. And the Soul said, "This is fine. Now I'm a bigger bird and I can fly higher." But before long, an animal came along and consumed the bird. The animal couldn't fly, but it could run very fast. So the Soul said, "I think I'll learn mobility on the earth." It discovered that the new form was strong, and it lived a long time in this form. Eventually, though, the form passed from the earth, and the Soul discovered itself in a new form—in the form of a man.

Through many lifetimes in human form the Soul discovered it had greater freedom than ever, even though it couldn't fly in this physical form. It realized the reality of itself. It realized that it had always been a Soul and that it had had all these other experiences. It realized that it had experienced all these other things, but had never really been any of them, that it had always been just what it was—a Soul, a part of God. It discovered that the strength of the Soul is far greater than the physical strength of the beast, and it found that its beingness is far more magnificent than the most magnificent earthly monarch. It discovered that its kingdom is neither on nor of the earth. So after many lifetimes it said, "I don't belong here," and it just dropped that physical form and moved directly into the Soul realm—its home. And the Soul was greeted regally; it entered royally and sat on the throne because it was the king of its own principality. That is the allegory of the Soul's evolvement.

The reality of the Soul's evolvement is more complex, but the story tells the essence of it. Within our universe, there are five planes, or realms, which we call the lower planes or negative planes. In this sense negative does not mean "bad," but rather, negative like the pole of a battery. A battery has negative and positive poles, and together they create the charge that is the power. In a similar way, the planes of existence have negative and positive poles.

The "negative" planes or realms are as follows:

The etheric realm—related to the unconscious level of man's consciousness

The mental realm—related to the mind of man

The causal realm—related to the emotional level of man

The astral realm—related to the imaginative level of man

The physical realm—related to the material substance of man's experience.

The physical level is the densest level. The Soul, expressing through various forms, may incarnate on any of these realms at various points in its journey. The Soul's experience on any negative realm other than the physical is more restricted or limited to that particular realm. But through the form of the human on the physical realm, the Soul's awareness is multidimensional and it has the unique opportunity of experiencing all negative realms simultaneously.

Not only can the Soul, through the human form, experience all the negative realms, but it also can directly experience the positive realms that exist beyond the negative. The first of the positive realms is the Soul realm. This is the first level where the Soul is consciously aware of its true nature, its pure beingness, and its oneness with God. There are also many ascending realms of pure Spirit above the Soul realm. They are all involved in the greater, more conscious realization of Soul and Spirit and God, until the Soul eventually dissolves its individuality into its greater oneness with the supreme God of all. These realms of pure Spirit really defy explanation in physical vocabulary; they must be experienced to be known. There are no words—it can only be said that they do exist and that it is everyone's potential and everyone's heritage to someday know of them in direct, conscious experience.

The Soul has its home in the Soul realm. That is the realm from which it has come. In many senses, it is a stranger to the lower or negative realms, and there is always within it the thrust to return to its home, to return to the realm of positive Spirit. The Soul incarnates in the lower/negative realms to gain the experience of those parts of God. Coming down through the lower levels, it picks up the form or "body" of each realm: etheric, mental, casual, astral and physical. Each form is heavier and denser than the one before. The physical form is the final body that is picked up and is also the densest. With the physical form come several levels of consciousness:

An unconsciousness (where memory is stored, where dreams may originate, and where many behavior patterns become automatic habits);

A mind (used to record events and record and play back information);

Emotions (where energy is generated and stored to be used as directed); and

An imagination (the expressions of which may be

positive or negative, and may enhance or block one's experience).

As the Soul takes on these different aspects, which are all reflections of the negative realms, it remains as the one positive aspect among all the negative (again, not bad, but negative). The Soul becomes the weakest part in the physical form because its job is to experience the lower realms through the physical form.

The physical form also comes equipped with:

A conscious self (which gets up in the morning, drives the car to work, reads the newspaper, studies the reports, talks to friends, etc.);

A basic self (which controls the bodily functions, directs the body in well-learned habit patterns, and much like a four or five-year-old child, asserts its desires and wishes upon the conscious self); and

A high self (which functions much like a guardian, directing the conscious self towards those experiences which will be for its greatest good, having knowledge of the life destiny of the physical form and attempting to fulfill it).

The conscious self is the "captain of the ship" and can ignore or override both basic self and high self. For the most part the high self will act in the best interests of the Soul's progression and evolvement; it will direct the human consciousness into those experiences it needs for its "education." The basic self will act primarily to preserve the body. It will resist anything that will harm or hurt the body or cause destruction to itself. The conscious self is the part that is most apt to get caught up in the illusions of the imagination, mind, emotions, and glamour of the physical world, creating situations that delay the Soul's evolvement.

When the human consciousness inflicts itself upon another human consciousness—when it creates harm, hurt, pain, etc., through physical action, thought patterns, verbal expression, dishonesty, deceit, financial fraud, emotional control patterns, or any other way— it is held accountable for that and will be given the opportunity to clear the action and bring it into balance. No one has the right to harm or hurt another, in any way. When that happens, the action must be balanced; it is the law of cause and effect. If you cause imbalance, the effect is that the imbalance is returned to you, as its creator, and you get to make it right. This, in essence, is the action of karma. It is a just and fair action. And it is the creation of karmic situations that institutes the action of reincarnation.

As a human, a Soul starts by incarnating once onto the physical realm, into a physical form. If that form could walk through its life here in perfect balance, creating only peace and love and harmony, it might complete and free itself from this realm and earn the opportunity to continue its evolvement on higher realms. But when the Soul incarnates into physical form, it is usually inexperienced in the ways of this world. The consciousness sees all the glamour, the illusions, the attractions of the world—the pleasures— and gets sidetracked. It is all a part of learning. So as it goes through its life plan, it is apt to create imbalance. Then when the time comes for the body to die, there are often karmic situations that have never been cleared or balanced. Thus, the Soul, at a later time, embodies again onto the physical realm so that it can clear its debts, right the wrongs, and bring balance and harmony. But if the consciousness again gets caught up in the illusions and the glamour, it may end up creating more karmic situations so that the Soul must again embody to clear them. And so on.

At some point in time, the consciousness will come into an understanding of this process, will learn to be a responsible creator, and will learn to place its value and its concern on those things that are positive and spiritual in nature rather than on the materiality of this world. In this way the consciousness begins its evolution back towards God, fulfills its past karma, stays free of accruing more karma, and liberates itself from this world. It is everyone's heritage to know the divine nature, to experience the joy and freedom and perfection of the Soul.

The Soul, in itself, is both positive and negative. It is complete in its energy pattern, just like its Creator is complete. But, when it decides to come into a physical form, it orients itself more towards one or the other polarity, male or female. It may say, "I'm going to come into the earth this time as a male." The high self, then, who works with the Soul, will go to the repository of basic selves and get a basic self that will be able to bring a body into the correct form. The basic self will begin to form the male body. The Soul will embody, at the time of birth, into the form as a male expression, but its energy cycles are still complete within itself because the Soul is perfect and complete.

The polarity of the body may feel the need for the balance of the opposite polarity and so it will seek out a mate, a companion, someone with whom it can exchange energy and feel complete. The male form expresses primarily a positive polarity; the female expresses a negative polarity. When male and female come together in the sexual encounter, the energies are exchanged; in essence, the battery is charged. People who are working with the high spiritual energies recognize the completeness of the Soul—and that recognition is their "Soul mate."

When you recognize that the Soul is perfect and complete, you have found your "Soul mate." The Soul does not look for a mate; it is perfect. It is the lower levels of consciousness that look for a mate, that seek to complete themselves. When you recognize that you are complete, then you will really have no need for the boundaries of this world. And this is what is often called self-realization. It is freedom!

All Souls were created at one "time." In God's "time" they have always been, but they have chosen different occasions to incarnate on this planet and gain their experiences. So each Soul is not equal in its progression and development, even though all are equal in the higher reality. Also, the time patterns between incarnations (or embodiments—you incarnate on the planet only once; your next lifetimes here are re-embodiments) may vary. There is no true average time between embodiments. So, although all Souls were created simultaneously, one may have experienced physicality more than another. One person may be experiencing their fiftieth lifetime here while another may be experiencing their hundred and ninety-fifth. That will make considerable difference in each one's awareness of Spirit and in each one's expression.

Over the eons of time on the planet, there have been many races of people. Each race is a different experience, a different consciousness. It is all "one" spiritually, but there is a separate consciousness within each race. You may not acquire the experience to know all of God in all his dominion unless you incarnate through all races. You may incarnate as a red man or woman one lifetime and learn it and never need to come back into that consciousness, or you may come in one lifetime as black or brown or white or yellow and learn it and never need to come back in that consciousness. It would be rare, however, to complete those experiences in one lifetime. When you get down here on the planet in all the levels of karmic fulfillment, it becomes difficult to fulfill all conditions in one lifetime.

Before you incarnate on the planet, you are in consciousness on some other realm living another existence. Then, for whatever reason, it becomes time for you to incarnate on the physical realm. Keep in mind that it is the nature of the Soul to experience all levels and conditions of God. Thus, the earth experience is part of the Soul's evolution into the greater consciousness of God. Before you re-embody you meet with karmic counselors or masters (known as the karmic board) to plan your life on the planet within high degrees of possibility and probability.

At this time of planning you choose your parents, you choose the talents and abilities you will have, and you choose those things that you and the karmic counselors decide will be best for you to further your spiritual progression. You also set up the situations that will bring you together with people in relationships that will give you the opportunity to fulfill karmic debts from your past existences.

It is the Soul's nature to incarnate onto the physical plane to gain experience, but it is the action of karma—the creation and the releasing of karma—that perpetuates the action of re-embodiment. Many people have lived hundreds of lives on earth and are still in the process of attempting to gain an understanding of karma so they can release themselves from the wheel of incarnation or embodiment, realize the freedom of their Soul, transcend this realm, and know the higher realms.

Before incarnation/re-embodiment you have free will and you exercise it; after you incarnate, you have free choice. Before you incarnate, you set up many possibilities; after you incarnate, you choose which of the possibilities you wish to follow. It is very complex and complicated to lay out all the variables that you can possibly enter into in your lifetime. It is so complex that if you attempted it with a computer, it would probably be inadequate to do what can be done by the masters of the karmic board who know, down to the most minute detail, what has happened through all of your existences. They sit with you, and then they sit with the Souls of your potential parents and family, and these patterns of your existence are worked out through many generations.

One metaphysical group says that an incarnation pattern is one hundred and forty-four years. They are setting forward a generalization that you will live on the planet for about one hundred years, and then, at your physical death, you will live about forty-four years in another realm before you re-embody back to earth again. The plan is approximately one hundred and forty-four years; however, within that cycling, you may break free much sooner; you may fulfill and work through your karma more quickly. But usually the karmic reactions that you set in motion will proceed for about one hundred and forty-four years.

Within your karmic pattern, for example, the counselors may set up actions whereby you work with the pattern of patience. In a former situation, you may have been very impatient with people and cut them off short, possibly by way of their heads. Because you created this action, you're going to have to enter into situations where you won't necessarily lose your head physically, but you will be experiencing impatience and losing your head in other ways, maybe through emotions or temper. The action may be symbolic rather than physical. You will enter into these situations to learn to become patient. It may be set up so that the one person who keys this off for you is someone from a previous lifetime who was a receiver of your action. Perhaps he will be your father this time. Before you re-embody you agree to the action and the conditions because it is fair that he gets the chance to balance the action.

In situations of this sort, it is possible that when the child incarnates, the father will see the child and experience a recall (not often on the conscious level) of the past life, and kill the child. This has happened. Usually, though, it doesn't happen because the "father" will give the "child" the opportunity to balance and fulfill the action. He must allow the action. These opportunities are so perfect. If you ever do something that is inflicting on another and play the little mental game of. "Oh, nobody knows; I can get away with it," think again. You're not getting away with anything. The Soul records it all and holds itself responsible for it all—in perfection and in justice.

Reincarnation is not negative, as a lot of people would like to believe. It's a very positive, progressive philosophy: if you don't make it now, you get another chance. What could be better than that? Everyone is working for awareness of the inner consciousness, seeking first the kingdom of God within and then seeking God in the outer reality. And everybody wants to reach heaven. But if you were told you were going to die in two weeks, you'd probably say, "Oh, God, no, I don't want to die. I want to stay in this misery." With that attitude you will, either now or later. You must be extremely careful of how you place things towards yourself because, being a creator and having divine essence within you, that which you create will be returned to you. You will be held responsible, as the author of the creation. It comes back to you.

The interesting thing is that within the Movement of Spiritual Inner Awareness, through its teachings, you can break the incarnation wheel. There are specialized techniques that are known to the people in MSIA who are courageously and consciously seeking for the uplifted experience. It can be difficult because often people may do their meditations, their spiritual exercises, their contemplation, or their upliftment of themselves for five minutes of the day, and for the other twenty-three hours and fifty-five minutes of the day put themselves down and lock themselves into the bondage of what we call the planet earth.

The temptation to focus on the negative of this level is very strong. However, with the inner support that comes from doing spiritual exercises and other spiritual practices, people are re-directing their focus to going back home to God.

2

The RULES *along the* WAY

We are each an extension of God and, as such, we have certain attributes in common with God. One is the power of creation. Part of our experience on the physical plane is to become a consciously aware and responsible creator, and to create those things that are positive in nature.

People create with emotions, thoughts, words, and actions. We can create misery, hurt, fear, revenge, etc., or we can create happiness, harmony, confidence, and joy. Everyone makes these choices many times each day. The things that you place in your mind as your "wants" and your desires, the things that you dream of and create in your imagination, become realities at some point, on some level. It is wise, to say the least, to be careful of the images you create and to which you give energy. But as long as you are going to place out a desire or a pattern of wishful thinking, you might as well place out the one that you really want. Is it God consciousness? Is it the higher realms, the Soul awareness?

What does a Soul look like? It could look like a purple ball or a white or gold one. It could look like the picture of a master, a picture of Jesus or Buddha or Krishna. As you put that image in front of you, it can start erasing the energy from the lower wishful thinkings that you have created, like the ones for the new car, the great sex life, the money, etc. You can program out the lower desires and start placing higher ideals in front of you. Your mechanisms for success will start pulling you right into the ideal. You can just assume you're going to reach it, because if that's what you keep in front of you, you will.

The Bible says, "As a man thinketh in his heart, he becomes." That really expresses a lot of truth when perceived from the mystical consciousness. It works both ways—positive and negative. You may say, "The thing that I feared most has come upon me." That would certainly make sense because the thing that you fear most, you think about. You give energy into it. You dwell on it and think: "What would happen if...?" and you create that which you fear and it appears. You create it. You bring it forward. Then you say, "Why me, Lord?" If you can get Him to communicate, the Lord may answer, "Why not? You created it; you're responsible for it." You might just as well take a deep breath, mark it up as an experience and a lesson, and go on. In reality, there is not much else you can do. Learn all you can from every experience and just go on.

Let's look at a situation. Suppose one of the things that you have brought forward karmically to work out is getting too emotionally involved with your loved one. When you love someone, you may want to breathe their air for them, digest their food, and make sure their heart beats just right and that the blood circulates in just the right places. You see this type of love often in mothers' and fathers' love for their children. They want everything to be so perfect for them that they try to protect them from life itself. It cannot be done. As much as you love people and try to bring their lives under your control, it just cannot be done. You feel that they are not living their lives the way you would like them to, and then you feel hurt and rejected.

Rejection is one thing I think everyone could do without. What happens when you feel rejected? You turn your thoughts in and you start going back inwardly to emotional patterns. You do not intellectualize. You may think you do, but you don't. You take the mind and add emotions to the thoughts. You mess up your thinking and circle your thoughts around. You

send out thoughts of hurt and frustration and bitter-
ness, and you bring them right back down through the
stomach. It really becomes self-pity time: "Woe is me. I
feel so sorry for me. They don't understand. They hurt
me. They don't do what I want them to do, what I need
them to do." These thoughts come out emotionally
charged, and then they come right back around and hit
you in the stomach. You will feel your energy drain off
as you feel this rejection. You may push the feeling of
rejection right down to the creative center of life, and
then when your loved one wants to come close and
make love with you, you say, "No way! Now, how do
you like feeling rejected?" So you deny them and
produce a karmic situation.

The karmic situation is produced from the dishonesty and the deceit accompanying the action, not
necessarily by the action itself. An honest approach
would be to say, "Look, today you said something that
hurt my feelings, and I really felt rejected and upset. So
it's going to be very difficult for me to make love with
you and feel good about it." Your partner will probably
say, "Wow, what did I say that hurt your feelings?" You
might say, "It was that comment about me being
overweight." And your partner may say, "Honey, I was
just kidding. I was teasing. I didn't mean anything. But,
you know, I've been putting on some weight l a t e l y, so

maybe we could start watching our diet a little more." This is being honest; this is communicating. This is clearing the air. These things are very important.

If you communicate honestly and keep the air clear between you and those people you live and work with, you will probably be staying pretty free of karma. It is when you let the little hurts, resentments, injustices (as you perceive them), and irritations build up that you are creating karma.

Many times people come together in a marriage or in a family to help one another work through karmic situations. It is interesting that you have karma only with yourself, not necessarily with other people. Other people usually come into the situation to give you the opportunity to handle your karma. In family situations karma becomes so involved that we often say families share karma. For example, a young man and woman may get married in a situation where, before their marriage, she has run up rather large credit card bills. Before the marriage, the man is not connected to that action in any way at all. After the marriage, he is responsible for those debts. He shares her financial karma and the law may hold him liable for payment.

That is an obvious example. Most are far more subtle. Many people seem to have relatively few problems before marriage, but when they get married they seem to have quite a lot of problems and difficult situations for a while. Then everything settles down and seems all right again. It takes time for both partners to adjust to new karma, to new karmic situations. Once they do, everything seems calmer again. So the family learns to work together and support each other through the times of trouble. If they get good at working with each other, they can actually work through karma more quickly because they will have more love to support them.

There will be times in your life when there will appear to be more karmic situations to handle than other times. That can be true. Every life has cycles and changes that come with the cycles. When there are times of heavy changes, it seems that there are many situations to handle. At other times, there appears to be more of a plateau; things just flow along easily without apparent turmoil. Both times may be right and proper and normal.

It is important to learn to accept and work with whatever is going on, without placing out too much in the way of judgments or self-recriminations. When you accept, it is easy because accepting is not resisting; it is letting things pass through and saying, "Thank you, Lord, for another wonderful day." When you can do this, it becomes so much easier to break free of the karma. **It is important to remember that you do not have to agree with something to accept it. You can disagree with the situation and still accept that that's the way it is.**

Handling karmic situations is like playing "jacks." You have your hands full of jacks, and you can spread them out and decide which game you want to play. You can play any game you want, but you have to pick them up. You can pick them up one at a time, and that is easy. Almost everybody can do "onesies," although it may take a long time to pick them up. But you never try for "allsies" until you've accomplished onesies, twosies, threesies, etc. Then, when you have done all the easy ones, you have to go on to something more complicated, like "put them in the basket." You bring forward a little different skill, which tunes you up a little more. And when you have mastered that, you go on to something like "over the fence" and you learn to master that.

Children's games can really be a lesson for us. Life is very much like a game. It is for keeps, but keep it a game. If you land in the wrong square, you go to jail, and you stay there until you can get a hundred dollars. Then you can get out, go back to "go," and start all over again. But the trick is to know when you are through with the game; then you can put it away and go on to something else. The trick is not to get so caught up in the game that you think you are the game. You are not the game. You are much more than the game. You are much more than your present karmic situation. You are much more than the personality you express this lifetime. It is just something you play out until you are finished with it. Then you let it go, release it, quit playing, and the karma is released.

As long as you are living in any of the lower/negative realms, you have some karma. If you had no more karma, you would leave the lower realms and be established on the Soul realm or higher. Even though you have karma here, you can keep your own house in order, taking care of things immediately as they appear on the scene. When something happens that really disturbs you, get up instantly and release it. If it is with another person, go to that other person and clear it. If it is something within you, go to work with yourself to change it and bring it into balance so that you are happy and comfortable with yourself. If it is on the job, talk to your boss and get it cleared or look for another job. If you learn from the disturbance, you will be free from it. If you do not learn, the experience will come around again and again, to give you another chance.

Problems are beautiful because every time you accomplish or overcome a problem, your wisdom and your knowledge grow. Every time you overcome something, you grow. The problems give you strength to go further. The earth is a classroom and everyone here is a student. The experiences that come your way, the problems that come your way, are your lessons. So every person you meet is your teacher. If you can keep that in mind as you are going through your day-to-day activities, you may be able to make some tremendous changes and really grow in your awareness very rapidly. You keep learning and progressing through each experience so that you can graduate, because if you fail, you are going to have to repeat the grade. And if that is what it takes, that's okay, too.

Karma can be created in several ways and through seemingly infinite situations. Basically, any action, emotion, thought, or word that is put forth in an out-of-balance manner may cause karma. If you become very angry and strike your child, that may very well create a karmic situation. Later you may find yourself apologizing, which clears the karmic action. But if the child has done something it should not do, a "punishment" may be the way that you make the child aware of its error so it can understand it. If you punish the child in love and discipline, not out of anger, you have created no karma, nor will you feel it necessary to apologize. You are merely helping the child to learn.

Much of this action has to do with attitude. It can make a big difference. You will bring many karmic situations to yourself through misuse of your emotional nature. You might think that if this is so, you will have karma the rest of your life. That may be true, but you will be a day older whether you work to clear your karma or not, so you might as well work on it. If you feel anger, if you feel hate, if you desire revenge, if you feel guilt or any of the other negative emotions, you bring karma to yourself. You bring it in and you hold on to it—and you will be held accountable for it.

The Soul is perfect; the personality is imperfect. But since the Soul has contracted to experience the physical realm with a particular personality and consciousness, it will re-embody to fulfill the karmic situations accrued by the consciousness, by the personality. The personality usually brings about karma through overindulgence. When you get so angry you are out of control, when you get so emotional, so upset, that you cannot control your tears and your sobs, when you get so drunk that you cannot remember or control what you do, when you get so spaced out on drugs that you are not in control—these situations bring karma to you. And probably more than any other single thing, the guilt you feel after these overindulgences will bring karma to you.

If you cheat on your wife, that may bring a karmic situation. However, it might be relatively easy to clear and balance it. But if you feel guilty, you can lock that karma in to yourself for a lifetime, or longer. If you have a child and give that child up for adoption, that may be a clear action. You may accrue no karma for that action. But if you feel that you should not have done it and you feel guilty, you can make it a karmic situation. If you become pregnant and decide to have an abortion, that decision and situation may be free of karma. But if you feel guilt and remorse and "beat yourself around the block" because of the action, you can produce a karmic situation. It is, really, very much a question of attitude.

There are many, many experiences on this realm. Many of them are not inherently "good" or "bad," but the attitude with which they are carried out may very well create a value judgment, which, if judged "bad," may create guilt, which will create karma. It is important to watch your attitude and keep it as neutral as possible.

The idea of karma, of creating and fulfilling karma, is incredibly complex. The planes and levels on which to create and fulfill karma are endless. If you multiply all of those by all of the situations, relationships, and attitudes that can create and fulfill

karma, you have what appear to be infinite possibilities. You have to learn to recognize, and then bypass,
every one.

Many times, karmic situations are both created and
fulfilled in one lifetime. Think of a situation where a
man marries a woman with whom he is very much in
love. He thinks she is the greatest girl in the world,
gives her everything, treats her like a princess...and
finds out that she is unfaithful to him. Her unfaithful-
ness causes him tremendous anguish and pain, and the
marriage eventually ends in divorce. Several years
later, she marries again. And she is tremendously in
love with her new husband, thinks he is the greatest
guy in the world. Then, after a while, she finds out that
he is being unfaithful to her. She is getting the opportunity to experience what she caused to be experienced. In the first marriage she was the cause, and in
the second, the effect. Really, she is lucky. She is
getting to balance the karma this lifetime. If it were not
balanced this time, it would be balanced another
lifetime. Nothing is overlooked.

If you, through deceit and lies, caused someone to
go to jail unjustly, you may find yourself at some
future point imprisoned for a crime that you did not
commit. If you then accept what is happening and
learn all you can from the experience, you will balance

and clear the karmic debt. But if you go into the expressions of hate, anger, and revenge, you will perpetuate your karma and get to experience it again and again until you learn to bring yourself into balance with it. You might not experience "imprisonment" as a physical prison experience. You might find yourself "trapped" in a job you can't stand and are not able, for some reason, to change. You might find yourself "trapped" in a family situation or in a marriage. There are a lot of ways to be imprisoned.

When you begin to understand karma, it is interesting to know that some actions which appear to be "bad," may be actions of fulfilling karma and therefore right and proper within that framework. For example, let's say that in a previous lifetime, a mother abandoned her child and left it in the hands of people who did not really care for the child. Because the mother refused to accept and handle her responsibility for the child, the child grew up unloved, abused, misused, and leading a very unhappy, embittered life. The child re-embodies at some point, grows up, and has a child of her own—which happens to be her mother from the previous life. She may feel no love for her baby and may abandon it, giving it the opportunity to have the same experience and learn what it is like to be abandoned and unloved.

People who observe this might be apt to judge the mother for abandoning the child, when in actuality she is only fulfilling the karma and bringing to the other consciousness the experience that is necessary to free it from the karma it had created in that other lifetime. Unless you can read the karmic records and see what is within each person's heart, it is best not to judge actions that appear to be cruel or unusual. It may be an action that is fulfilling a karmic debt.

Sometimes, also, a situation that is fulfilling and clearing karma may appear very similar to a situation that is creating more karma. But there is a difference. If you experience a situation that really gets you shook up and upset and doubtful about what is actually happening, you may still be growing and moving right along your spiritual path. The best way to determine if this is so is to look for that little feeling of joy somewhere inside, even through the upset and the pain and the anguish. If there is still a part of you that says, "It's okay because I'm learning and growing," then you are probably clearing a karmic situation. And there may be other times when you are upset and shook up and you will know you are not growing or learning.

At these times, you are not releasing or clearing karma; you are just going through things that you have promoted, and you will probably add to the original upset the judgment of being disturbed and upset with yourself for creating the situation. Then you will get to handle that later. Even if you are involved in a situation that is not a situation of karmic release, do not judge yourself or put yourself down. Just go through it, get out the other side as rapidly as possible, and go on. Don't look back; it doesn't help. Don't burden yourself down with guilt and remorse that you are going to have to handle later. Just let it go.

When a situation is a karmic release manifesting itself, you will feel, within all your nervous irritation, a calmness. In all of your imbalance, you will feel a balance. This is not double-talk, as much as it might sound like it. It is more of a description of what is happening simultaneously on two levels of your consciousness. One level is ranting and raving and screaming, and the other level is saying, "Go ahead, get it out of your system so you can move on. You let it build up; now clear the air. Put everything right while you have the chance. Finish it up so we can move ahead."

Clearings are often very important, especially if you have let irritations and misunderstandings build up within your consciousness. You must be free to reach into the spiritual realms and into God consciousness.

You cannot be restricted by the resentment of how your boss treated you a year and a half ago or last week. You cannot be restricted by your husband's remark about the dress you made. These things must be cleared and balanced. You can do it two ways:

1. You can go to the person with whom you had the misunderstanding and talk to them about it, tell them how you felt, communicate honestly and openly, and clear the air that way; or

2. You can simply release it within your own consciousness, just let it go, place no more energy out that way, place no more concern with it, and erase it out of your consciousness.

Either way will work. An attitude that will help is just to realize that people are doing the very best they can all the time, considering what they are working with and where they are in their own progression.

If your boss yells at you, maybe you shouldn't take it personally. Maybe he and his wife had a big fight the night before and she threw him out of the house. Maybe you remind him of someone that he has had a difficult time with in the past, and some part of his consciousness is expecting the same situation. Maybe you and he have a karmic relationship where the job of each of you is to learn communication and love in relation to the other. There are so many possibilities.

There is very little use in trying to figure out exactly which possibility applies. You might assume that there is a reason for his behavior, that it is important to both overcome the block (whatever it is), and not create a bigger block by putting out resentment, resistance, and other negative emotions. With honest communication you can recognize where he is coming from, gain an understanding of his motivations, and come into a position of empathy and love.

When you reach into a higher consciousness, you come to the realization that we are all one Spirit in many different manifestations. If you strike against anyone, you strike against yourself, and that action returns to you. If you curse someone, that curse returns to you. It may be this lifetime or it may be a future lifetime, but it returns.

What you put out is returned to you. You might want to look very carefully at the actions, the words, the thoughts, and the emotions that you put out, to make sure that they are the kind of things that you would want returned to you. Often there is a comparatively large time gap between the instigation of an action and its result; the cause and the effect. This is one reason why it is difficult for people to recognize the relationship between the cause and the effect. If you steal a car and go joyriding when you are sixteen, and twenty years later a bunch of kids steal your brand new Cadillac and wreck it, it may be difficult for you to see the connection. But it is there. It is just your action being returned to you.

You may work out karma on the astral realm (which appears to be very similar to the physical realm) if there is some reason that it cannot be worked out here on the physical. This might be done in the dream state, and you would bring back the memory of it as though it were a dream. Or it could take place in an awake state. Consider this example.

Several years ago I was talking to a medical doctor who related to me a very interesting experience. He told me that he had recently delivered twins. I said, "Well, so what? That's your job." He said, "No, I don't mean that I delivered a woman of twins. I delivered twins; I had twins." I asked him to explain more, since that sounded like a medical phenomenon, to say the least.

He told me that a woman who had been a patient of his for some time had become pregnant. About the time she was three or four months pregnant, she and her family moved away. At some future point the doctor went into severe labor pains. That was the only way he could describe it. Not only did he feel like he had delivered one child, but he felt like he had delivered two. This experience was recorded in his office; his nurse was aware of all this because he was not sure whether to call an ambulance and go to the hospital or just stay at the office.

He was pretty sure he was not having a heart attack because the pain wasn't in that area. For a while he thought he might be having an intestinal attack of some kind, but he was aware that it probably was not that, either. He was in tremendous pain for quite awhile. After the pain let up he was talking to his nurse, and said, "You know, I hate to say this, but I feel like I just had twins." She laughed and said, "You know, it isn't unusual, Doctor, for a father to go through sympathy pains when his wife is having a baby." He said, "But my wife is not having a baby; she's not even pregnant."

The experience ended, and they both sort of forgot about it until he heard from his former patient telling him that she had delivered twins. He checked the time, and his experience was within that same period of time of her labor and delivery. He feels certain, and there is certainly evidence to verify it, that he had tuned in and had an affinity with this woman experiencing this birth pattern the way that she experienced it.

In checking into his past life experiences, it did show one lifetime where he, as a female, had produced a karmic situation in a very similar pattern but had not resolved it. This present lifetime he was involved in consciously breaking the incarnation pattern, so it was important for him to have this experience, to finish up the karma, and to tie up the loose ends so he could go freely. Being male this lifetime, he could not have the experience of childbirth directly, so he experienced giving birth as a psychic function.

He said, "It was real. It was painful." Yet the woman who was delivering the twins did not have pain because she was under an anesthetic. He had taken some aspirin and finally had given himself a shot of codeine to stop the pain, but it didn't help. It did not stop the pain because it was not a physical pain; it was a psychic pain. That experience of pain was part of the karmic release. It was necessary to the experience. It helped him to have the conscious knowledge of what the karmic situation was and why he had experienced it, but the conscious knowledge was not so necessary to releasing the karma. Just having the experience and going through it is what was important.

Often things happen to people that do not seem to have explanations. For example, a child is born deformed or blind or deaf, and it causes great distress within the family and often within society. The action of karmic fulfillment explains many of these instances.

Let's look at another example. In ancient times, people were sometimes punished by having a hand cut off or a tongue cut out. If the one who performed these punishments got caught up in the experience to the point that he did it unnecessarily or for pleasure or unjustly, even according to their laws, he might very well find himself in his next incarnation being born without a hand or arm or unable to speak. He would be allowed that experience to gain the understanding of what it was like, and thereby fulfill the karmic debt.

If a person experienced a form of sadism in one life, that person might find himself the child or the spouse of a sadist the next lifetime (or a later one). The possibilities are complex and infinite and depend on many, many variables of situation, attitude, intent, etc. But the law of karma says that there will be perfect justice.

When you know of the law of karma, you know that if something happens to you that you think from your present consciousness, is unfair, you can just let it go. You know that if it is unfair, the person will be held accountable for that, through Spirit. You do not have to do anything. You do not have to seek revenge. You do not have to try to get even. You do not have to think about it. You do not have to hang on to the experience at all. You can learn whatever you can from it, let it go, and go on to your next experience.

If you don't enter into the negative expressions of revenge, hurt, despair, etc., you will keep yourself open and present for your next experience, which may be a beautiful one. If you do go into the negative aspects, you may block the next experience that is coming forward. It is very important to keep moving in your consciousness and not to hang on to old hurts and pains. Let them go as soon as possible and get on with the business of living. You will find your life much more enjoyable and much happier.

3

LEARNING *the* LESSONS *and* GOING BACK HOME

People who choose to study in MSIA work with the Mystical Traveler, a spiritual consciousness that exists throughout all levels of God's creation. It resides within each one of us and is a guide into the higher levels of Spirit, the greater reality of God. The Traveler can assist a person in clearing karma (balancing past actions), and its work is done inwardly, on the spiritual levels.

Students have the opportunity to break free of the wheel of incarnation this lifetime, to become established on the Soul realm, to walk in freedom while they are here, and upon their physical death, to lift up in consciousness to the high realms of pure Spirit. This is the promise the Mystical Traveler extends; this is the way of Soul Transcendence that is taught.

As the expression of the Mystical Traveler Consciousness, part of my job in relation to the MSIA students is to establish them in Soul consciousness. To do this there is much assistance given to help them fulfill their karma and teach them to walk free of accruing additional karma. Often, when someone first begins working within MSIA, they will appear to have more "problems" than they did before because they will be working through their karma faster. Not only past karma, but the karma they create day-to-day will be returned to them very quickly—within hours or days, instead of years or lifetimes. If a person "blows up" at himself or another person and is "fuming" inside, he may go out to take a drive and find that fifteen minutes later the radiator blows up and steam fumes out of the car. Instant karma. Cause and effect. He handles it; it is over, it's clear. This is very fast. He can continue right on.

Relationships that have been slowly deteriorating for years may suddenly collapse, forcing a confrontation, forcing the people to communicate and clear the air. The relationship may re-establish itself and be better than ever, or it may be over. In either case, it becomes clear so that both people have more freedom.

The Light, which is the energy force MSIA students are taught to work with, originates in the high, positive realms of pure Spirit. Its energy is positive. Its force can only be used in love and for the highest good of all. It cannot hurt, harm, or destroy. But it can stir up negativity that has remained dormant for a long time, bring it up into consciousness, and cause it to be cleared. On the word level, you can think of the Light as an acronym for Living In God's Holy Thoughts. In reality, the Light is the indescribable essence of God.

When people first become consciously aware of these teachings and express an interest in them, they are taken during the "night travel" (the sleep state when the physical consciousness is at rest and the higher consciousness is free to travel into the other realms) and are shown the records of their past karma. They are also shown the karma that they will be working through this lifetime. At this point, they either decide to work with the higher energies, to follow this path of spiritual unfoldment, and to work consciously to fulfill their karma, or they decide to continue their life pattern with a lesser consciousness of the spiritual realities and without the direct guidance of the higher consciousness.

If someone chooses to work consciously with the Mystical Traveler Consciousness and to learn the path of Soul Transcendence, there is much protection and grace extended. No harm will come to the students unless they deny the teachings or block the work—and even then it would only come from the negative power. When the Mystical Traveler works with you in higher consciousness, it takes you during night travel into the Soul realm, into the realms of pure Spirit, and then back down through the lower realms of illusion to help you work off the karma you have accrued. The five lower realms, including the physical, are lands of illusion. Experiencing them is like being in a fun house with distorted mirrors and clear glass panels—you can really get twisted around and lost in the experience.

When the Mystical Traveler takes you into the higher realms, it is like suddenly being lifted straight up out of the fun house and being able to see clearly where all the different paths are, where the maze begins, where it ends, which paths are the dead ends, and so forth. Everything becomes very clear, and you can see which path you want to take. When you come back into physical consciousness, as you awaken in the morning, you may forget the specifics of where you were during the night travel and what you learned, but the essence will remain with you so you know you are on the right path.

When you reach into the Soul realm (the sixth realm) and above, there is no karma to work out there. You are in pure Spirit. This is why the Mystical Traveler teaches Soul Transcendence. We reach into Soul and then come back down through the lower levels of Light—but still in Soul consciousness. That way, when you work off karma, you work it off from a pure state. It is like walking through the manure pile in hip boots. The Soul protects the consciousness. The Soul is involved within the form of each realm so that you do not accrue more karma, but you are still able to do the work.

You are working off karma here on the physical realm. But you also have karma to work off in the other realms. There is karma of the astral realm, the causal realm, the mental realm, and the etheric realm. You can work out your karma here on the physical realm by confronting your karmic situations. When you come to a situation, you know you can either fight or run. Ultimately, however, you must confront every-thing. You cannot turn away. When you have confronted the "problem" or experience and exercised your wisdom of choice, you can move from it. But you must come to grips with it.

When the Traveler works with you, you have the opportunity to work off physical karma on the other realms during night travel. Perhaps you were a reckless driver and were the cause of several accidents in the past, but you were never directly involved. The Lords of Karma may have a rather serious accident on your karmic plan, a lesson to teach you responsibility on the road. (Remember this is a plan you helped create and have agreed to fulfill.) During the night travels, if we see that it is not necessary for you to have the total experience physically, we may be able to alter it and allow you to experience the car wreck in another realm.

You might bring back the memory of the car wreck through a very vivid dream experience—the kind where you hear the brakes screaming, feel the car going out of control, hear the sound of metal scraping against metal, feel the impact as you crash, feel the body being thrown through the air, and wake up in a cold sweat, shaking all over from the experience. That has been your lesson, and it has been real enough to bring home the point that you must drive more carefully. You have fulfilled the karma, but through the grace extended to you, you do not have to experience it physically and handle all the physical consequences of a major car accident.

If you have experienced a difficult time with your parents, moved away from home, and left unresolved many problems between you, you may find that some morning you awaken with the memory of being with your parents in a dream and telling them of your love for them and sharing with them your present happiness. Your parents may call that day just to say they love you very much. These things happen. It is no coincidence—though it may appear to be. During the night travel, during the dream state, you may be releasing the hurts and resentments that you have carried for years.

The consciousness of the Traveler works on every level of consciousness, on every realm of Light—and works with you totally to release you from the negative realms. To reach Soul consciousness and be established in the Soul realm, to break the wheel of incarnation, you must fulfill all karma on all the lower realms—astral, causal, mental, and etheric, as well as physical.

The astral realm may be heavily laden emotionally because it is so close to the earth. It is also the realm of the imagination; so when you are working on the astral, you may have tremendously imaginative dreams. When you get into the causal realm, you often find that the dreams are of a highly emotional type, and the karma involved is highly emotional, also. The dreams of the mental realm will reflect the mental aspect of consciousness; you may dream that you are attending classes and learning many things. You may not remember the dreams of the etheric realm at all, as they relate to the unconscious. If you do, they will be more like impressions, not like clear images. For the most part it is your imagination and your emotions that are used to work out karma.

Many times in the dream state you create illusion fields around yourself that will seem very real to you and provide the framework through which you work out your karma. You may not be aware that it has been created through illusion, and it can scare the daylights out of you. You can really frighten yourself with what you have created. Many of your fears that you create during the day become "reality" on the astral realm. Probably most of your nightmares are just you meeting up with those "monsters" you have created. It is all illusion. The instant you shift your focus and deny their existence, they are gone. Part of your training during the night travel is learning to discern reality from illusion. When you have perceived and confronted all illusion, you will find that only the Soul is left and you will be home free.

4
MAKING *it a*
JOYFUL JOURNEY

Much of the trick of keeping free and clear of karmic relationships with yourself has to do with attitude. There are very few things within our world that are inherently "good" or "bad," except as we label them. If you are to stay free and clear, it becomes important to place out as few judgments as possible, to maintain as neutral an attitude as possible. If you've had a "lousy" day, and you call it a "lousy" day, be aware that you are placing that attitude of "lousy" back on your consciousness because you're going to harvest that.

It is valuable to evaluate your position every day. If you were going to buy stock, you would probably want to evaluate the current market to decide which stocks to buy. And, of course, you would want to buy "good" stocks. But what is "good" stock and what is "bad" stock? Naturally, good stock is the stock that's going up and bad stock is stock that's going down. "Good" and "bad" are judgments; "up" and "down" are descriptions of what's happening. So you really want to buy stock that's going up. But keep in mind that the stock that's going down today might someday go up; and then it would be "good."

"Good" and "bad" are not absolutes, and therefore they might be called illusions. All that is really happening with a stock is that it may be going up or down. If you say a stock is "bad" and it starts back up, it may be difficult to get on the bandwagon and take full advantage of its beneficial rise because you will already have labeled it within yourself, and you will have to defend your position. For you, it will never be good. If you just observe which stock is up and which is down and follow the trends, then you are in a free position, ready to take advantage of any opportunity you perceive with any stock on the market. You have not blocked any possibility and the channels are all open.

A very similar process happens inside of you with other things. If you label some things as "bad" and then they start shifting and bringing forth something for you, it may be difficult to participate in them because you have placed yourself against them. If you start a new class and flunk your first test, you can either label yourself as a "failure" and label the teacher as "no good," "too hard," or "not fair," or you can simply be aware of the fact that you received a failing grade on the first test and use that experience and that knowledge to point your direction towards more study and more preparation for your next test.

If you label yourself as a "failure," you are creating your failure, and it may be difficult to pass the next exam, the next, and the next. If you label the teacher as "no good," it may be difficult to meet the assignments with a positive attitude and achieve any success in the class. However, if you just use the failing experience to become a better student, it may be very easy to pass the exams and the class.

Labeling and name-calling can have many ramifications within your consciousness. If you've called your spouse a dirty, no good, son of a gun, or some other name, it can be very difficult to turn around the next minute and express love towards that person. It is really difficult, then, to walk up and say, "I love you." You have to get your negative creation out of your system. You vent your spleen or go away somewhere and take a walk. You get drunk, or do something else. Why? What happens?

When you call your spouse a name you have judged against the love that you have placed out for them, and it hurts you. You have rejected your love, and you've rejected the person to whom it went. You are hurt because you've rejected yourself, and it takes time to get over the judgment against your love. Perhaps I should say your affection, because if it were really love, that love would flow no matter what. The level of affection often moves into areas of hurt and rejection. So if you would have joy and peace and harmony, place within yourself the seed of pure love—not affection, unless the affection comes as a result of the love. Then the affection is nice because it is tempered and balanced in wisdom and in joy.

Affection often brings about control patterns (or attempted control patterns), depression, rejection, and hurt. Everybody has been there before. You know where that is. As long as you keep placing that seed back inside of you, that is what you are going to keep bringing forward. But you don't have to re-create that infinitely. You can change it anytime you wish and bring forward pure love.

You can just start changing right where you are. Do you have a bad temper? Look at it; evaluate it. Let's look at temper. Temper is a self-defense mechanism. If someone attacks you, your temper kicks in and you lash out to protect yourself or your loved ones. You place within yourself the seeds of self-rightfulness, and no one else can invade that position. Then you have to attempt to defend your position of self-rightfulness, and if that is a false position, then you have cheated yourself from experiencing what another person can bring forward and share with you.

There are very few things on this planet that cannot be looked at in a matter-of-fact, straightforward way. If you look at every point of view from a clear consciousness, you can see value there. This is why you can be right, your mother can be right, your wife can be right, the newspaper editorial can be right—all people can be right from diverse positions. This doesn't necessarily mean that you have to function from their position of rightfulness, but you can recognize that how they see things is right for them. You have the right, however, to live your life the way you see it.

You have a potential to learn from everyone you meet. There is truth in everyone's expression, just as there is probably illusion in everyone's expression. If you just observe and stay neutral and objective in your evaluations of the circumstances, you can bring to yourself those things that are presently of value to you. You can bypass those things that are not of value to you at the time without blocking the possibility that they may be valuable to you in the future. You just let all experiences flow through, and what you want, you bring in. What you do not want, you bypass.

Here is an analogy: if you were visiting a diamond mine and someone very joyfully said, "You can have as many diamonds as you can get off the conveyor belt in thirty seconds," you would see some interesting reactions. Some people would start grabbing with one hand and then with the other. It is also foolish because once you have a few diamonds in each hand, that's it; you can't grab anymore. But if you put one hand on the conveyor belt and just steer the diamonds towards you for thirty seconds, you'll get a lot more. After all, if you're going to be greedy, you might as well be good and greedy—and smart and greedy. Don't be a nitwit about it. Get all you can, so that when the thirty seconds are up, you don't walk away saying, "If I could have just picked those things up faster." If you regret, you are living in the past. To live in the "here and now," you say, "I did the very best I could. I got all I could." And you leave it at that.

While you are here on this planet, get all you can in the levels of your experience, in the levels that bring forward your own unfoldment. As soon as you grab for one thing, you are going to lose something else; it is going to go by you. That is why you keep yourself open and flexible, and you just keep moving. As a new experience comes in, you are right there to learn from it. You're not off in your mind regretting what happened in the past or daydreaming about what might happen in the future; you are "here and now." Keep moving your position constantly into the "here and now."

There is nothing permanent on the physical level. Everything is in a state of change. Keep flexible on this level. When a building starts to fall, don't stand there to show you are right. Get out of the way. Move. One of the things that is fairly permanent on this level, for this lifetime, is being a man or woman. Some things are just sort of there, and it's nice to cooperate with them. Other things are more changeable. I am not really talking about the physical things, like the color of your eyes (though even those can be changed by wearing colored contact lenses or staying up for a few nights in a row). Such a change may not be permanent, but do you think your eye color now is going to be permanent? We'll see what color they are in a hundred and fifty years.

Many levels are changeable. People say, "You changed your mind." That is why you have a mind; so you can change it. That is why you practice changing, so you can change when it is necessary. If you try to hold to a static position, you may find out that in your strength of trying to be self-determined and not bending even the slightest bit, you crack and fall. Then you cry out in pain and suffering. If you have the wit to see a tornado coming and get out of the way, you will survive. It can become difficult when you say, "I'm just going to stay right in the middle of this wind. I don't care how hard it's blowing. I'll be strong." When you find you cannot withstand it, you come back again and again, learning to bring yourself into the flow of life. It is important.

One of the lessons to learn here is to be flexible. That is not necessarily being "wishy-washy." There is strength and wisdom in being flexible. It takes great strength to change your position when that position is no longer defensible and to say, " I defended a position that is now not defensible." If people say you're wrong to change, you can answer, "If that's the way you label it, okay. I just can't defend that position now; that's where I am. And I am now moving my position." If they tease and ridicule, don't give in to their pressures and social blackmail—don't go back to your old position to "show them." Demonstrate your strength by maintaining the change, the new position.

Consider this example. A husband comes home and wants to take his wife out dancing to his favorite nightspot. She doesn't really want to go. So he coaxes her into going. She gets dressed and he says, "Are you going to wear that dress?" She says, "Now I'm not even going." That is blackmail; she went back to the old position to show him. She was ready to go and have a good time, but just to show him, she went back to the old position. With that kind of attitude, nobody can show you. You can't even show you.

Usually when you think you are hurting someone else, you're really hurting yourself. When you are tired of it, you will change. If you like that feeling of misery, go ahead and enjoy yourself. Hang right in there. Are you sick of it? Do you want to change? Then change. If the wife wants to go out driving instead of dancing, and the husband feels happy about doing that, then that will be good for both of them. They can go and enjoy life together. But if he's going to sit in the car and be depressed because he wants to be dancing, if he wants her to be aware of his depression and punish her because she won't do what he wants to do—she is foolish if she goes along with it.

No one should have to enter into someone else's artificial standard of what they think should be done according to their depressed state. Too often people plant the seeds of, "I'm self-rightful and authoritative, so I'll tell you." If they do not know the answer to your question, they may think, "I can tell you something that I don't know because I know you don't know—so I know you'll never be able to prove me wrong." It happens often. The problem is that someday the other person finds out the truth and says, "You lied." That seed you planted is then yours; the consequences of your lie are yours.

You cannot live with liars or cheats. You cannot trust them. You do not know what they are going to do or say next. You won't recognize the truth if they do tell it because they have confused it with so many lies. You will not be able to trust them with the things that are sacred to you, but maybe you should keep those things to yourself anyway. You do not have to trust anybody if you trust yourself.

Stay within the realm of honesty and truth within your own consciousness. By doing this, you can lift people around you. You can transmute their dishonesty, if you want to put forth the energy. When people tell you something, you can say, "How about that! That really sounds good," without jumping into their information. You look at it carefully and consider whether their information relates to you. Be sure you are going to be happy about harvesting what you are planting. Or are you going to be entering a situation that will cause guilt and cause you to come back to this realm and work it out again?

Do not enter into any situation that causes you even a little twinge of feeling, "Oh, I wasn't all that honest."

That's guilt. No matter how thin you slice baloney, you still have baloney; and no matter how "small" the guilt, it is still guilt. The degree of it is important—that's for sure. Because the more guilt you feel, the more you intensify your existence; and the more intensity you place on this existence, the more you lock yourself into the force field of this planet. Then you have to come back into that force field and evolve again.

One of the biggest keys is to watch your attitude. Remember, the stock isn't "good" or "bad," which is a judgment. It is just presently going up or down, which is an evaluation. All you have to do is evaluate a situation. Do not place a judgement, a moralistic value, on it. In the Soul, there is no morality; there just is. The personality has morals. It will judge, put out self-rightfulness, call you dirty names, and maybe hit you in the face. But the Soul is attempting to get through all these levels of the seeds and weeds you have planted.

Sometimes it takes a long time for people to go back through all the acreage in which they have sowed their wild oats and do all the weeding and the clearing of the land and reclaiming of the good soil. And do that they must before they can even start from "go" and move forward on their spiritual path. If there are too many weeds, you may find yourself not making it this time around. Even so, you are on your way because you are dropping away those things that are not needed. You do not have to add more.

A lot of people are trying to add more: to read more, to do more, to work more, to play more. Other people are realizing that they have to unlearn much that they have learned: in school, in church, in society, in parental relationships, and so forth. It is the time for some real Soul-searching, to discover what works for you and what does not work for you. Wisdom is using those things that work for you, for as long as they work for you, and letting go of the things that are not working for you.

The new pattern is to release those things that are on you—old habits, negativity, attachments, desires, whatever—and stand free. In standing free, you will move automatically from this existence into the next where your freedom can take you. If you don't get high enough in your freedom, you will come back to earth again to gain more freedom in order to go higher. You will choose to come back because, from the spiritual vision, you can see how you can do it so perfectly, experience so much, learn so much, and go so high.

You come back and you may lose much of the vision as you get caught up once more in the illusions of this world. But it is very nice to know that, regardless of how you perceive your life or how you perceive the cosmos, it's all in its right place, doing the right thing, performing absolutely correctly. Even that little sense of depression, that little thought of suicide that you may have had, was an awakener for you. You awakened from that into greater awareness, and now you can lift higher.

The Soul embodies on the earth to gain experience. When you have had an experience, you do not have to repeat it, unless you re-create it. If you learn from everything that happens, if you use everything as an opportunity to learn and to lift yourself, you will be earning your freedom. So learn from the experience of your life. Set your goals high and go for them. Do not let anyone or anything sidetrack you. Create only the very best things for yourself.

5

PLANNING FUTURE JOURNEYS

I would like to tell you how to prepare for your next incarnation. If you are going to be born again in any way, shape, or form, you might as well know something about it. Some people who are working within the teachings of MSIA will break through the pattern of reincarnation, but many will be returning. It is self-evident that not everyone will take the high philosophies and work with them. They will not move into the mystical consciousness this lifetime. They will dwell in the psychic, material worlds, in the worlds of negativity. But knowledge of the truths of reincarnation will be of assistance to them. Many will start by just recognizing that they are not the only form of consciousness around.

You, in this present moment of your existence, have arrived at this point due to certain processes that have taken place within your consciousness, your unconsciousness, or your higher consciousness. It is not necessary to go into all of these levels—only to recognize that these are the planes of consciousness and that they do have a profound effect on your spiritual unfoldment. Everyone attempts to continually break forward into something new: "A new year! Hallelujah! I'm going to go on and really grow." So you make New Year's resolutions. Yet your expectation level and your reality level do not often match. The people who have a beautiful year are those whose expectations and reality match, and as a result, they feel balanced.

If you were going to change something inside of you and come back as another personality, who would it be? What would it be? Just reflect on that. What would your next life be like? What do you want it to be? Look on the inner screen of your mind for the answer. What is it that you see? What do you really want? Do you see greater wealth, a greater sensitivity to music or the arts, a position of political power, a religious leader "saving" the masses? Do you see yourself playing the violin or the piano? Do you see yourself as a doctor or a teacher? What are the qualities that you would need inside of you to be that person? In what location of the world would you have to live in your next incarnation? What would the environment be like? You may come up with a blank. If so, you had better look deeply into your existence right now because you may start pulling blanks into your present lifetime.

It is best to move your consciousness someplace, to put it in a direction, and to keep your eye on the target. You will find yourself pulling to the target, and as you get closer and closer, you will be able to modify, to lift it or lower it or move it right or left. You will be able to adjust your sighting so that you come into your goal. As you sit back and contemplate a future existence, you can program that into a future existence. There is a danger in this if you are close to breaking free of incarnation patterns, because if you program it, you'll come back to complete it. So, if you are working within the structure of MSIA, you might want to place any contemplation of a future lifetime within the context and the protection of, "Lord, if this is for my highest good ..." That way you can protect yourself. If it is for the highest good that you do not reincarnate, then you will not block that possibility.

Remember when you were very little and wanted to be a fireman or a train engineer or a mounted policeman? You might start putting a "deflect" on those desires, because the desire patterns that you created (even though you may have forgotten about them) can come back in. Then you say, "Oh, God, what have I done to myself?"

As you learn how to alter your consciousness, you can evolve a new lifetime for yourself at any moment, right here and now. You can adjust and change, but you have to have the wit to move towards the new, which means letting go of the old. When you have had enough of creating the negative things—unhappiness, isolation, loneliness, and depressions—and when you are sick and tired of being sick and tired, you can alter and change.

As you move through experiences in your life, pay very close attention to what is taking place within you and around you. Observe what actions and reactions, what thoughts, what daydreams, what words, etc., create negative results—either physically, emotionally, financially, mentally, creatively, or unconsciously—in yourself or in others. Observe those actions that produce positive results. With conscious direction, control and discipline, move your expression more and more into that which creates positive results within yourself: better health (physical, mental, emotional), greater wealth, and more happiness. That is the path to freedom.

As you create positive effects, you will be dissolving past karmic bonds and will not be creating additional karmic debts. You will be moving into freedom. This is why I am so very careful with everyone I meet. I state over and over that I am responsible only for what I say and do. If someone tries to involve me in their illusion, you will hear me say, "I'm not part of that; I'm not involved in that." I do not let anyone get me into anything. You have the same right. You have the same freedom. If someone tries to get you to do something that does not feel clear to you, just let them know. Say, "I don't feel clear doing that. I don't feel comfortable. I'm not going to be involved. If you want to do it, go ahead; I'm not part of it." And go your way. You are responsible for what you create. It is wise to be careful.

6

KNOWING *your* RESPONSIBILITIES

Dharma, or duty, is being of service in an unselfish way. Your dharma to yourself and to other people is very, very important. In many ways, dharma could be considered the positive aspect of karma because if you are fulfilling your dharma, you will also be fulfilling your karma.

First of all, we have a duty to people who are younger than we are; we have a duty to prepare a place for them in this physical world. Whether or not they are our own, we have a responsibility towards them. Spirit resides in all, and we have a duty to that Spirit. Then we have a duty to our friends and acquaintances, people our own age. We have a duty not to judge them. Judgement produces karma, not dharma. Our dharma to our peers is to love and support them and to work with them in harmony.

Then we have a duty and a responsibility to the people who are older than we are. We can respect their wisdom and their longevity. The Bible says to honor thy father and mother that your days may be long upon this plane. It means more than the father and mother of your flesh and blood; it means people older than you. We respect them for their experience. Maybe they don't have all the wisdom in the world, but they have had experience that is valid. You can tap that experiential level in them and draw it forward, and that can become your experience also. You can experience it through them. It is the same as if you went out and did it. There is little difference because the experience is the same inside of you. This is tremendously valuable, if you use it.

You have a duty to the society in which you live. When you take care of the children, yourself, your friends, and the older people, that duty to society is automatically handled; it is already happening. Then your duty to your nation and your hemisphere is fulfilled, and everywhere you go, you are then performing your dharma. When you have completed all of these, you have done your duty to God. Some people believe that going to church on Sunday constitutes their duty to God, and they don't do anything the rest of the week. That may be hypocrisy. Dharma is a living, ongoing, breathing, daily manifestation. It is a way of life.

You have a duty to your employer. He (or she) has invested himself with you, trusted you to carry out a job for him. Your dharma is to hold that trust sacred and to do all you can to complete the job correctly. Your dharma to your friends is also to hold sacred their trust and love in you, and to love and support them in return—not to malign or misrepresent or betray them. Your duty to yourself is to keep free and flowing, to accept what comes your way, to work with it, to learn from it, and to progress continually upward.

As you learn to accept responsibility for small things and to fulfill them well, you will be given greater things. It is a similar process at your job. As you demonstrate to your boss that you can be trusted, that you can handle the job he gives you, he gives you a better job with more responsibility in a position of greater trust. As you demonstrate you can handle that job, he gives you another promotion. Life is like this. As you demonstrate your ability to handle your responsibilities, you are given greater responsibilities and opportunities.

Those people who are going to break free of their karma this time, those people who are going to release themselves from their karmic debts and from the lower realms of negativity, must indeed demonstrate that they are ready to handle their responsibilities, their duty, their dharma. It is a twenty-four-hour-a-day, seven-day-a-week job. There are no vacations either, but the rewards are certainly worth it. The job requires total commitment to honesty, truth, duty, and love, a continual demonstration of those qualities, and eternal vigilance so that you don't miss anything. It is not easy, at least not at first. After awhile, the rewards start coming in, and you will find that you wouldn't have it any other way. As you create love, harmony, happiness, joy, and peace, these qualities will be returned to you. Then the world will become an easier, happier place in which to live.

As you give, it is returned to you on this level and on other levels. Don't be too concerned about this level. It has many illusions; things here are not permanent. They fall apart, decay, and change. Place your concern and your values in the spiritual realms. The things of this world come and go. Property deteriorates and falls apart. Bodies get old and fat, or old and skinny. Hair falls out. Machines break down. The Bible says, "Seek ye first the kingdom of heaven and all things will be added unto you." This is real and true. The truly religious or spiritual person who performs his dharma responsibly, who follows spiritual laws of acceptance, understanding, empathy, perseverance, love, joy, creativity and manifestation, will do very well on this physical realm, as well as gaining spiritual freedom. The more one gives, the more one receives. The two go hand in hand.

Choose wisely your direction because you may find yourself being held to your choice, especially if that choice is a destructive attitude. If you choose a positive attitude, that is beautiful; you won't mind being held to that all day long because you are going to reap the land of milk and honey, the happy feeling, a deep joyfulness.

With the joyfulness comes responsibility and knowledge. Knowledge always comes from beauty. When you see something beautiful, it attracts something inside of you, and that thing inside of you says, "Oh, that's so pretty." You want to know more about it. Finding out more about it is knowledge; and knowledge becomes awareness. So your knowledge has always been based upon your perception of something beautiful. What one perceives as beautiful, of course, another may not, because beauty is in the eye of the beholder. As you perceive an essence of beauty and then seek for knowledge, you find that there is a love within. This love is the divine essence, which is God.

Ultimately, seeking after beauty, knowledge, and awareness finds you back in God's graces. You cannot help but make it. People who struggle in this lifetime are playing the fool. It is not a struggle; it's a game. If you are punishing your loved ones because of a level of disturbance within you, then you have corrupted yourself and your love for those you care about. But if inside of you there is only love, it does not matter if you say outwardly, "Now, knock that off!" because that is the role you play to accomplish the desired result. Inside of you, you are not that role; you are something else. This something else is what we call the spirit, the love, the beauty, and the perfection of each person's Soul consciousness.

You will awaken—every one of you—to the knowledge that you are divine, that the Soul within you is directly an extension of God, and that it is your heritage to move in consciousness from the lower worlds of negativity into the heavenly worlds of Spirit. That is the spiritual promise which is pre-ordained in the journey of every Soul.

Here are some of many other books by John-Roger,
available through bookstores everywhere:

Forgiveness: The Key to the Kingdom   ISBN 0-914829-62-9

Inner Worlds of Meditation   ISBN 0-914829-45-9

Loving Each Day — Reflections on the Spirit Within
ISBN 0-914829-26-2

The Power Within You   ISBN 0-914829-24-6

Relationships – Love, Marriage and Spirit ISBN 0-893020-05-3

Sex, Spirit and You   ISBN 1-893020-03-7

The Spiritual Family   ISBN 0-914829-21-1

Spiritual Warrior: The Art of Spiritual Living
ISBN 0-914829-36-X

The Tao of Spirit   ISBN 0-914829-33-5

Momentum: Letting Love Lead   ISBN 1-893020-18-5

When Are You Coming Home?   ISBN 1-893020-23-1

*The Movement of Spiritual Inner Awareness (MSIA), founded by
John-Roger, offers a wide range of study materials and courses. For
more information, or to order books or tapes, please contact us at:*

MSIA
P.O. Box 513935
Los Angeles, CA 90051-1935
800/ 899-2665
servicedesk@msia.org
www.msia.org

About the Author

A teacher and lecturer of international stature, with millions of books in print, John-Roger is an inspiration in the lives of many people around the world. For over three decades, his wisdom, humor, common sense and love have helped people to discover the Spirit within themselves and find health, peace, and prosperity.

With two co-authored books on the *New York Times* Bestseller List to his credit, and more than three dozen self-help books and audio albums, John-Roger offers extraordinary insights on a wide range of topics. He is the founder of the nondenominational Church of the Movement of Spiritual Inner Awareness (MSIA), which focuses on Soul Transcendence; Chancellor of the University of Santa Monica; President of Peace Theological Seminary & College of Philosophy; and founder of the Institute for Individual and World Peace and the Heartfelt Foundation..

John-Roger has given over 5,000 lectures and seminars worldwide, many of which are televised nationally on his cable program, "That Which Is," through the Network of Wisdoms. He has been a featured guest on "Larry King Live," "Politically Incorrect," "The Roseanne Show," and appears regularly on radio and television.

John-Roger continues to transform lives by educating people in the wisdom of the spiritual heart.

CPSIA information can be obtained at www.ICGtesting.com
Printed in the USA
BVOW08s0509200616

452420BV00002B/2/P

9 781893 020139